SRA OPEN COURT READING

A t

Te on

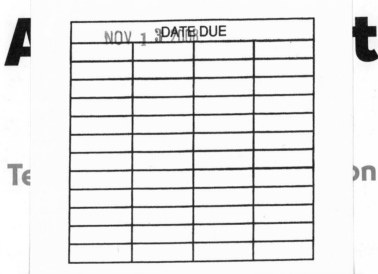

www.sra4kids.com

SRA/McGraw-Hill

A Division of The McGraw·Hill Companies

Send all inquiries to:
SRA/McGraw-Hill
8787 Orion Place
Columbus, OH 43240-4027

Printed in the United States of America.

ISBN 0-07-571669-0

2 3 4 5 6 7 8 9 MAZ 07 06 05 04 03 02

Table of Contents

Introduction v

Unit Assessments

Unit 1
Teacher Directions 2A
Lesson Assessments 2
End of Unit Assessments 13

Unit 2
Teacher Directions 20A
Lesson Assessments 20
End of Unit Assessments 29A

Unit 3
Teacher Directions 35A
Lesson Assessments 35
End of Unit Assessments 42

Unit 4
Teacher Directions 44A
Lesson Assessments 44
End of Unit Assessments 50

Unit 5
Teacher Directions 54A
Lesson Assessments 54
End of Unit Assessments 61

Unit 6
Teacher Directions 63A
Lesson Assessments 63
End of Unit Assessments 68

Unit 7
Teacher Directions 70A
Lesson Assessments 70
End of Unit Assessments 74

Unit 8
Teacher Directions 75A
Lesson Assessments 75
End of Unit Assessments 80

Assessment Records
Class Assessment Record 82
Student Assessment Record 92

Open Court Reading Unit Assessments

The *Unit Assessments* are an integral part of a complete assessment program that aligns with the instruction in *Open Court Reading.* The assessments are intended to show how well students understand the skills addressed in each unit and how well they can apply those skills. The following are examples of the types of assessment found throughout the units.

ASSESSMENT	FORMAT	SCOPE
Lesson Assessment		
Warming Up	Multiple Choice	Understanding of concept words such as those for colors, numbers, and shapes
Phonemic Awareness	Multiple Choice	Understanding of phonemic awareness skills developed in the lesson
Comprehension	Multiple Choice	Understanding of comprehension skills developed in the lesson
Book and Print Awareness	Oral	Understanding of book and print awareness covered in the lesson
End of Unit Assessments		
Listening	Multiple Choice	Listening skills developed from unit to unit
Vocabulary	Multiple Choice	Vocabulary skills and strategies developed in the unit
Grammar, Usage, and Mechanics	Multiple Choice	Understanding of grammar, usage, and mechanics skills introduced and practiced in the unit
Sounds and Letters	Oral and Multiple Choice	Recognition of sounds and letters in the unit

Assessment Guidelines

- **Professional Judgment.** Although *Open Court Reading* provides a full range of assessments, the teacher is the final judge of how many of these assessments should be administered and when they should be given. The following factors should be considered in making these decisions:

  - All students should be assessed for the most critical skills such as basic reading and writing skills. These assessments should be administered following the procedures described in this book.

  - Some skills are best assessed directly or using observation of the student in typical classroom situations rather than formal assessment measures.

  - Students who are lagging behind the class as evidenced by their assessments or other criteria should be given a chance to complete all the assessments. This will help the teacher identify the strengths and weaknesses of these students. In addition, the assessments themselves are a form of additional practice, particularly when the teacher is able to provide the students with any help they need to complete the assessments.

  - If students seem to be struggling with the assessments intended for the whole group, the teacher should not hesitate to administer them individually and provide whatever oral help is necessary. This accommodation is reasonable because it allows students to demonstrate their knowledge of a given skill they have been taught rather than assessing their developmental level or socioeconomic background.

  - Assessments may be administered to a student more than once if the student does not reach the recommended performance level. This is especially true of the individual assessments of critical literacy skills. These assessments measure students' understanding of skills such as alphabet knowledge that are the foundation of later learning. Repeated administration of these assessments plus additional instruction is the best way to ensure that students acquire these skills.

- **Diagnostic Tools.** *Unit Assessments* are diagnostic tools that can be used along with informal assessments to help determine when students need additional skill instruction. That additional instruction may be *Reteach* support for those students who may just need to go over the lesson once more or *Intervention* for those students who need even more support. *Unit Assessments* also help identify students who understand the skills well enough to use *Challenge* to push their abilities even further.

Assessment Records and Folders

One of the most important elements of assessment is organizing the data in a way that is convenient and usable for the teacher. ***Open Court Reading*** provides the following components to help keep organized records.

- **Student Assessment Record** summarizes all assessment information for each student to review with students and parents.

- **Class Assessment Record** summarizes scores on Lesson and End of Unit Assessments for the entire class. This allows the teacher to identify groups of students with similar needs. The students may then be grouped for targeted instruction, practice, or enrichment.

- **Cumulative Folder** provides an organizer for a variety of student assessments including ***Program Assessments, Unit Assessments,*** and other indicators of student progress. The assessment pages should be organized by date with the earliest work in the front of the folder. This organizational method will allow you to evaluate both qualitatively and quantitatively the progress a student is making.

- **Writing Folder** provides an organizer for student drafts, revisions, and writing presentations. The pages should be organized by date with the earliest work in the front of the folder. This will allow you to evaluate student written work both qualitatively and quantitatively.

Introduction

Teacher Directions

The content of this unit consists principally of readiness skills the students will need to move on to more formal learning in later units. The assessments and their administration methods are shown below:

Assessment	Method	Recommended Performance Level
Counting	Group	4/5
Counting	Group	4/5
Classifying and Categorizing	Group	3/5
Classifying and Categorizing	Group	5/6
Word Sequence	Individual	4/6
Rhyming Words	Group	4/5
Colors	Group	4/5
Shapes	Group	4/5
Differentiating Words, Numbers, and Letters	Group	5/5
Print and Book Awareness	Individual	9/12
Measurement Words	Group	4/5
Position Words	Group	4/5
Opposites	Group	4/5
Vocabulary	Group	4/5
Number Recognition	Individual	8/10
Letter Recognition	Individual	12/12
High-Frequency Words	Group	4/5
Alphabet Sequence	Individual	4/6
Words That Name	Group	4/5

Although all the assessments relate to the lessons in the unit, the following assessments are the most critical and should be administered to every student. In addition, these are the assessments that the teacher should re-administer if a student does not reach the recommended performance level.

Counting
Number Recognition
Letter Recognition
Alphabet Sequence
Print and Book Awareness

Name _____ Date _____ Score _____

UNIT 1 School • **Lesson 5**

Counting

[**Teacher:** This activity is about numbers. Look at each number. Draw a line under the picture that shows this many things.]

1. 2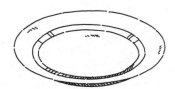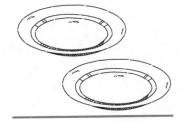

2. 7

3. 3

4. 4

5. 9

Unit 1 Assessment • *Counting*   Unit 1 • Lesson 5 **2**

LESSON ASSESSMENT

UNIT 1 School • **Lesson 5**

Counting

[Teacher: This activity is about numbers. Draw a line from each picture to the number that tells how many.]

1.

2.

3.

4.

5.

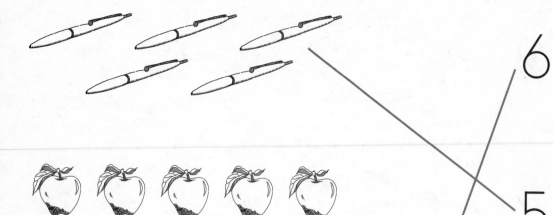

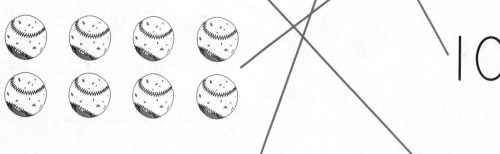

6

5

8

10

1

Counting • Unit 1 Assessment

Name _____ Date _____ Score _____

UNIT 1 School • Lesson 8

Classifying and Categorizing

[Teacher: This activity is about grouping things that are similar. Listen carefully to what I say. Draw a line under the answer you think is right.]

[Teacher: Which answer shows only things you would eat?]

1.

[Teacher: Which answer shows only things in which you travel?]

2.

[Teacher: Which answer shows only things you wear?]

3.

[Teacher: Which answer shows only things that fly?]

4.

[Teacher: Which answer shows only things that you read?]

5.

UNIT 1 School • **Lesson 8**

Classifying and Categorizing:
Numbers, Small Letters, Capital Letters

[**Teacher:** Look at the three columns. At the top of the first column is a number. That means all the things in that column should be numbers. I want you to cross out the things that are <u>not</u> numbers in the first column. *(Walk around the room and be sure the students understand what they are supposed to do. After the students have completed the first column, repeat the directions for the second column (small letters) and third column (capital letters).]*

9	b	K
c̶	g	F
2	3̶	k̶
6	d	G
7	h	A
E̶	L̶	4̶
5	f	D

Numbers total: _____

Lower-case letters total: _____

Upper-case letters total: _____

Phonemic Awareness: Word Sequence

Directions for the Teacher

This assessment is intended to be administered to students individually. Duplicate page 6B for each student you choose to assess. Write the student's name and today's date in the appropriate spaces. You will record the student's responses on this page.

Sit at a table that allows you and the student to work comfortably. You may find it easier to sit across from the student rather than beside the student.

Read the following directions:

Teacher: This activity is about first, middle, and last words. I will say three words and ask you a question about them. You will tell me the answer. Let's practice. The three words are *knife, fork, spoon*. Which is the middle word: knife, fork, spoon? (allow the student to answer the question) ***The middle word was fork.* Are you ready? Let's begin.**

Read the questions. Mark the box beside each question the student answers correctly. For ease of scoring, the correct answer is shown after the question.

After you have completed the assessment, record the number right in the spaces below the columns and on the STUDENT ASSESSMENT RECORD and CLASS ASSESSMENT RECORD. Place the completed page in the student's *cumulative folder*. If any students do not meet the recommended performance level, repeat the assessment after intervention or additional instruction.

UNIT 1   School • **Lesson 10**

Phonemic Awareness: Word Sequence

☐ The words are ***bird, fish, rabbit***. Which is the last word: bird, fish, rabbit? rabbit

☐ The words are ***crayon, pencil, pen***. Which is the first word: crayon, pencil, pen? crayon

☐ The words are ***bus, car, truck***. Which is the middle word: bus, car, truck? car

☐ The words are ***orange, apple, pear***. Which is the first word: orange, apple, pear? orange

☐ The words are ***bed, table, chair***. Which is the last word: bed, table, chair? chair

☐ The words are ***house, school, store***. Which is the middle word: house, school, store? school

Word Sequence total _____

UNIT 1 School • **Lesson 12**

Rhyming Words

[**Teacher:** This activity is about things that rhyme. Look at the pictures. Say the name of each picture to yourself. Draw a line under the picture whose name rhymes with the name of the picture in the box.]

1.

2.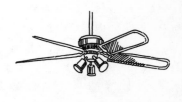

3.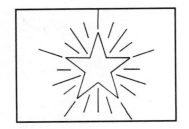

4.

5.

LESSON ASSESSMENT

UNIT 1 School • **Lesson 13**

Colors

[Teacher: This activity is about colors. Listen carefully to what I say. Draw a line under the answer you think is right.]

[Teacher: Draw a line under something that is usually green.]

1.

[Teacher: Draw a line under something that is usually yellow.]

2.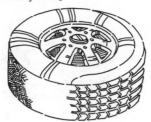

[Teacher: Draw a line under something that is usually red.]

3.

[Teacher: Draw a line under something that is usually gray.]

4.

[Teacher: Draw a line under something that is usually brown.]

5.

Name _____ Date _____ Score _____

Shapes

[Teacher: This activity is about shapes. Listen carefully to what I say. Draw a line under the answer you think is right.]

[Teacher: Draw a line under the shape that is different from the others.]

1.
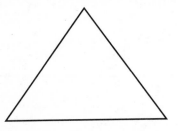  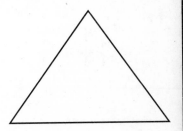

[Teacher: Draw a line under the circle.]

2.
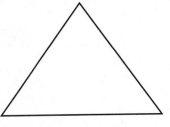  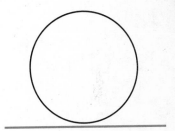

[Teacher: Draw a line under the square.]

3.
 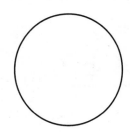 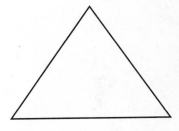

[Teacher: Draw a line under the triangle.]

4.
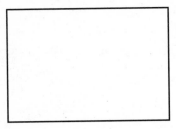 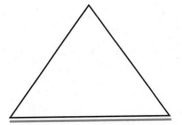 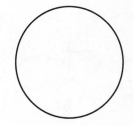

[Teacher: Draw a line under the rectangle.]

5.
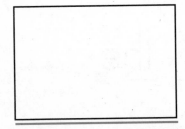 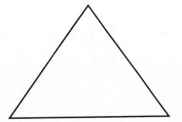 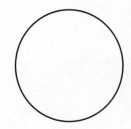

UNIT 1 School • **Lesson 15**

Differentiating Words, Numbers, and Letters

[Teacher: This activity is about letters, numbers, and words. Listen carefully to what I say. Draw a line under the answer you think is right.]

[Teacher: Look at the first set of answers. Draw a line under the answer that is a letter...a letter.]

1.

<u>d</u>　　　　　3　　　　　is

[Teacher: Look at the next set of answers. Draw a line under the answer that is a number...a number.]

2.

an　　　　　A　　　　　<u>2</u>

[Teacher: Look at the third set of answers. Draw a line under the answer that is a word...a word.]

3.

7　　　　　<u>here</u>　　　　　g

[Teacher: Look at the fourth set of answers. Draw a line under the answer that is a letter...a letter.]

4.

4　　　　　6　　　　　<u>F</u>

[Teacher: Look at the last set of answers. Draw a line under the answer that is a word...a word.]

5.

e　　　　　B　　　　　<u>the</u>

LESSON ASSESSMENT

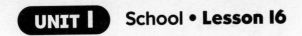

Print and Book Awareness

Directions for the Teacher

This assessment is intended to be administered to students individually. As an option, you may observe students during regular classroom activities and check the skills they demonstrate.

Duplicate page 10B for each student you choose to assess. Write the student's name and the date in the appropriate spaces. You will record the student's responses on this page. After you have completed the assessment, record the number right in the spaces below and on the STUDENT ASSESSMENT RECORD and CLASS ASSESSMENT RECORD. Place the completed page in the student's *cumulative folder*.

Sit at a table that allows you and the student to work comfortably. You may find it easier to sit beside the student. Put the *Big Book* *School* on the table with the cover down. Ask the student the questions below. Check each question the student answers correctly.

Name _____ Date _____ Score _____

UNIT 1 School • **Lesson 16**

Print and Book Awareness

☐ Show me the front cover of this book.

☐ Show me the back cover of this book.

☐ If you were going to read this book, how would you hold it?

(For the following three items, be sure the cover of the book or the title page is showing.)

☐ Point to the title of the book.

☐ Show me the name of the person who wrote the book.

☐ Now show me the name of the person who drew the pictures in the book, the illustrator.

(For the following questions, be sure the student opens the book to a typical two-page spread.)

☐ Open the book. Show me a page number.

☐ Point to a word on the page.

☐ How about a letter? Point to a letter for me.

☐ If you were reading this page, show me the word you would read first.

☐ Now show me the words you would read next. Move your fingers to show me the direction you would read the words.

☐ If you were reading this page, show me the word you would read last before turning to the next page.

Print and Book Awareness total: _____

UNIT 1 School • Lesson 18

Measurement Words

[Teacher: This activity is about words that describe things. Listen carefully to what I say. Draw a line under the answer you think is right.]

[Teacher: Which tree is the tallest?]

1.

[Teacher: Which of these is heaviest in real life?]

2.

[Teacher: Which box is the smallest?]

3.

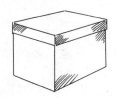  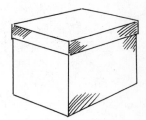

[Teacher: Which fish is the longest?]

4.

[Teacher: Which house is the shortest?]

5.

LESSON ASSESSMENT

UNIT 1 School • **Lesson 19**

Position Words

[Teacher: This activity is about position words. Listen carefully to what I say. Draw a line under the answer you think is right.]

[Teacher: Draw a line under the cat that is <u>beside</u> the chair.]

1.

[Teacher: Draw a line under the bird that is <u>over</u> the tree.]

2.

[Teacher: Draw a line under the butterfly <u>on</u> the flower.]

3.

[Teacher: Draw a line under the ball that is <u>in</u> the box.]

4.

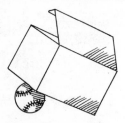  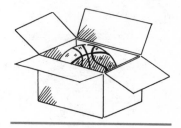

[Teacher: Draw a line under the man who is <u>beside</u> the truck.]

5.

UNIT 1 School • Lesson 20

Opposites

[Teacher: This activity is about opposites. Listen carefully to what I say. Draw a line under the picture that shows the opposite of what I say...the opposite of what I say.]

[Teacher: Draw a line under the picture that shows the opposite of up . . . the opposite of up.]

1.

[Teacher: Draw a line under the picture that shows the opposite of little . . . the opposite of little.]

2.

[Teacher: Draw a line under the picture that shows the opposite of hot . . . the opposite of hot.]

3.

[Teacher: Draw a line under the picture that shows the opposite of out . . . the opposite of out.]

4.

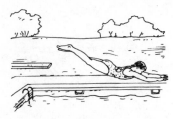  

[Teacher: Draw a line under the picture that shows the opposite of big . . . the opposite of big.

5.

 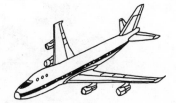 

Name _____ Date _____ Score _____

UNIT 1 School

Vocabulary

[Teacher: This activity is about words we learned before. Listen carefully to what I say. Draw a line under the answer you think is right.]

[Teacher: Look at the pictures. Which picture shows someone painting...someone painting.]

1.

[Teacher: Look at the pictures. Which picture shows a bus...a bus?]

2.

[Teacher: Look at the pictures. Mark under the squirrel that is second from the tree...second from the tree.]

3.

[Teacher: Look at the pictures. Which picture shows someone jumping...someone jumping?]

4.

[Teacher: Look at the pictures. Which picture shows a desk...a desk?]

5.

  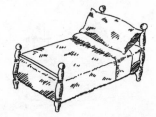

Vocabulary • Unit 1 Assessment

Number Recognition

Directions for the Teacher

Page 14 should be used to assess students' knowledge of numbers 1 through 10. This assessment is intended to be administered to students individually.

Duplicate page 14 in the student workbook. Write the student's name and the date on the duplicated page. You will record the student's responses on this page.

Sit beside the student at a table that allows you and the student to work comfortably. Have the student turn to page 14 in the student workbook; provide whatever help is necessary to ensure that the student is working on the correct page. **Do not have the student mark in the book.** This will allow you to re-administer the assessment, if necessary.

Point to a number at random and ask the student to name that number. Avoid pointing to the numbers in order. You should use a prompt such as "What number is this?" or "What is the name of this number?".

Continue the assessment as long as the student seems engaged. If possible, give the student an opportunity to respond to all the numbers. Discontinue the assessment if the student is distracted, is responding randomly, or makes five errors in a row.

Number Recognition *(continued)*

Use the following scoring conventions:

- Use the duplicated page to record the students' responses.
- If the student names the number correctly on the first try, circle that number.
- If the student names the number incorrectly, draw an X over the number.
- If the student makes an error then self-corrects, put a small question mark beside the number. Retest the student on this number after you have tested at least one other number. You may use the same procedure if a student hesitates for a long time before responding or appears unsure about a number.
- Do not allow the students to see how you have recorded their responses. Moreover, do not give them feedback about answers being right or wrong.
- After you have tested all the numbers and retested those for which the student provided an uncertain response, record the number right, the number wrong, and the number that remain uncertain in the spaces below and on the STUDENT ASSESSMENT RECORD and CLASS ASSESSMENT RECORD. Place the completed page in the student's *cumulative folder*.

Because number recognition is such an important skill, you should provide additional instruction and retest any student who does not reach the recommended performance level.

UNIT 1 School

Number Recognition

8   3   6

2   9

10   7   4

5   1

Number Right: ____

Number Wrong: ____

Number Uncertain: ____

Letter Recognition

Directions for the Teacher

Pages 15 and 16 should be used to assess students' knowledge of capital and small letter names for A through L. This assessment is intended to be administered to students individually.

Duplicate page 15 (capital letters) or 16 (small letters) in the student workbook. Write the student's name and the date on the duplicated page. You will record the student's responses on this page.

Sit beside the student at a table that allows you and the student to work comfortably. Have the student turn to page 15 or 16 in the student workbook; provide whatever help is necessary to ensure that the student is working on the correct page. **Do not have the student mark in the book.** This will allow you to re-administer the assessment, if necessary.

Point to a letter at random and ask the student to name that letter. Avoid pointing to the letters in alphabetical order. You should use a prompt such as "What letter is this?" or "What is the name of this letter?".

Continue the assessment as long as the student seems engaged. If possible, give the student an opportunity to respond to all the letters. Discontinue the assessment if the student is distracted, is responding randomly, or makes five errors in a row.

Letter Recognition *(continued)*

Use the following scoring conventions:

- Use the duplicated page to record the students' responses.
- If the student names the letter correctly on the first try, circle that letter.
- If the student names the letter incorrectly, draw an X over the letter.
- If the student makes an error then self-corrects, put a small question mark beside the letter. Retest the student on this letter after you have tested at least one other letter. You may use the same procedure if a student hesitates for a long time before responding or appears unsure about a letter.
- Do not allow the students to see how you have recorded their responses. Moreover, do not give them feedback about answers being right or wrong.
- After you have tested all the letters and retested those for which the student provided an uncertain response, record the number right, the number wrong, and the number that remain uncertain in the spaces below and on the STUDENT ASSESSMENT RECORD and CLASS ASSESSMENT RECORD. Place the completed page in the student's cumulative folder. If any students do not meet the recommended performance level, repeat the assessment after intervention or additional instruction.

UNIT 1 School

Capital Letters

I   D   F

C   G   K

J   A   E

H   B   L

Number Right: _____

Number Wrong: _____

Number Uncertain: _____

UNIT 1 School

Small Letters

f   d   l

k   b   g

c   i   j

h   e   a

END OF UNIT ASSESSMENT

Number Right: _____

Number Wrong: _____

Number Uncertain: _____

UNIT 1 School

Unit High-Frequency Words

[Teacher: This activity is about words you have learned. Look at each group of words and listen to what I say. Draw a line under the word I say.]

[Teacher: The word is *the*. Draw a line under *the*.]

1.

she   he   the

[Teacher: The word is *here*. Draw a line under *here*.]

2.

help   here   her

[Teacher: The word is *is*. Draw a line under *is*.]

3.

is   in   it

[Teacher: The word is *an*. Draw a line under *an*.]

4.

on   in   an

[Teacher: The word is *see*. Draw a line under *see*.]

5.

saw   see   sat

END OF UNIT ASSESSMENT

Alphabet Sequence Part I

Page 18 should be used to assess students' knowledge of the alphabet sequence. This assessment is intended to be administered individually. Duplicate page 18 in the student workbook and fill in the student's name and the date.

Sit at a table that allows you and the student to work comfortably. You may find it easier to sit beside the student. Have the student turn to page 18 in the student workbook. **Do not have the student mark in the book.** This will allow you to re-administer the assessment, if necessary.

Teacher directions: This page has some of the letters of the alphabet. Some of the letters are missing. I would like you to say the missing letters of the alphabet in the right order. Let's do the first row together. The two letters are *a* and *b*. What letter comes next in the alphabet? The letter *c* comes next, so I will write the letter *c* in the space. Do you understand what you are supposed to do? Now, I will read the rest of the letters. Tell me the missing letters in the order they appear in the alphabet. If you think about the alphabet song, it will help you.

After you have completed the assessment, record the number right in the spaces below the columns and on the STUDENT ASSESSMENT RECORD and CLASS ASSESSMENT RECORD. Place the completed page in the student's *cumulative folder*. If any students do not meet the recommended performance level, repeat the assessment after intervention or additional instruction.

UNIT 1 School

Alphabet Sequence

a b _c_

d _e_ f

_g_ _h_ i

j _k_ _l_

Alphabet Sequence total: ____

Alphabet Sequence • Unit 1 Assessment

END OF UNIT ASSESSMENT

UNIT 1 School

Words That Name

[Teacher: This activity is about nouns, words that name. Listen to the word I say. The word is in the box. Draw a line under the first answer if the word names a person, place, or thing. The first answer is "yes." Draw a line under the second answer if the word I say is not a person, place, or thing. The second answer is "no."]

[Teacher: The word is *school*. Does this word name a place? Draw a line under yes or no.]

1.    yes   no

[Teacher: The word is *read*. Does this word name a thing? Draw a line under yes or no.]

2.    yes   <u>no</u>

[Teacher: The word is *mother*. Does this word name a person? Draw a line under yes or no.]

3.    <u>yes</u>   no

[Teacher: The word is *run*. Does this word name a thing? Draw a line under yes or no.]

4.   yes   <u>no</u>

[Teacher: The word is *book*. Does this word name a thing? Draw a line under yes or no.]

5.    <u>yes</u>   no

END OF UNIT ASSESSMENT

UNIT 2 Shadows

Introduction

Teacher Directions

The content of this unit consists of readiness skills and those that reflect more formal learning. Also assessed are important listening skills that are the precursors to reading comprehension. The assessments and their administration methods are shown below:

Assessment	Method	Recommended Performance Level
Cause and Effect	Group	4/5
Counting Words in Sentences	Group	4/5
Picture–Text Relationship	Group	4/5
Drawing Conclusions	Group	4/5
Word Order in Sentences	Group	4/5
High–Frequency Words	Group	3/5
Word Length	Group	5/5
Vocabulary	Group	4/5
Fantasy and Reality	Group	5/5
Letter Recognition	Individual	12/14
Alphabet Sequence	Individual	4/6
Matching Capital and Small Letters	Group	26/26
Action Words	Group	4/5
End Punctuation	Group	6/8

Although all the assessments relate to the lessons in the unit, the following assessments are the most critical and should be administered to every student. In addition, these are the assessments that the teacher should re-administer if a student does not reach the recommended performance level.

Counting Words in Sentences
High-Frequency Words
Word Length
Letter Recognition
Alphabet Sequence
Matching Capital and Small Letters

Name _____ Date _____ Score _____

UNIT 2 Shadows • **Lesson 4**

Cause and Effect

[**Teacher:** This activity is about cause and effect. Listen carefully to what I say and the question I ask. Draw a line under the picture that is the best answer to the question.]

[**Teacher:** There was a big storm last night. The wind blew a tree down. Which picture shows what the wind did? Draw a line under your answer.]

1.

[**Teacher:** Jenny was playing baseball. She threw the ball too far. It broke a window. Which picture shows what caused the broken window? Draw a line under your answer.]

2.

[**Teacher:** Peter's grandmother took him to the zoo. He was very happy. Which picture shows what caused Peter to be happy? Draw a line under your answer.]

3.

[**Teacher:** Mr. Howard drove over a nail. He got a flat tire. Which picture shows what happened to Mr. Howard's car? Draw a line under your answer.]

4.

[**Teacher:** Rita worked in the garden all day. She was tired when she was finished. Which picture shows what made Rita tired? Draw a line under your answer.]

5.

Unit 2 Assessment • *Cause and Effect*

UNIT 2 Shadows • **Lesson 5**

Counting Words in Sentences

[Teacher: This activity is about words in sentences. Listen carefully to the sentence I say. Draw a line under the number of words in the sentence. The answers are 2,3, or 4]

[Teacher: How many words are in this sentence: Ben went home.]

1. 2 3 4

[Teacher: How many words are in this sentence: Hello, Ann.]

2. 2 3 4

[Teacher: How many words are in this sentence: Pedro can read.]

3. 2 3 4

[Teacher: How many words are in this sentence: This is my house.]

4. 2 3 4

[Teacher: How many words are in this sentence: The dog is brown.]

5. 2 3 4

Name _____ Date _____ Score _____

Picture-Text Relationship

[Teacher: This activity is about pictures and stories. Listen to the sentence I read and look at the picture in the box. Draw a line under the first answer if the picture matches the sentence. The first answer is "yes." Draw a line under the second answer if the picture does not match the sentence. The second answer is "no."]

[Teacher: A bird built a nest in a tree near our house.]

1.  yes no

[Teacher: Lydia is taking her dog for a walk outside.]

2.  yes no

[Teacher: Some fish are in a bowl that is on a table.]

3.  yes no

[Teacher: Mr. Johnson is washing his car.]

4.  yes no

[Teacher: Virginia wears a helmet when she rides her bike.]

5.  yes no

UNIT 2 Shadows • **Lesson 8**

Drawing Conclusions

[Teacher: This activity is about drawing conclusions. Listen to the story I read and the question. Draw a line under the picture that shows the best answer to each question.]

[Teacher: Cassie and her mother are holding long poles. They are walking toward the lake. What do you think they will do?]

1.

[Teacher: Cary and his father are in the kitchen. They have bread, cheese, meat, tomatoes, and lettuce. What do you think they will do?]

2.

[Teacher: It's a windy day. Some children are in the park. They are holding onto string. What do you think they are doing?]

3.

[Teacher: Tina is coming home. She has lots of cards and presents in her arms. Her mother is carrying part of a cake. Where do you think Tina and her mother were?]

4.

[Teacher: Ralph is talking to grandmother who lives very far away. How do you think he is talking to her?]

5.

Drawing Conclusions • **Unit 2 Assessment**

Name _____ Date _____ Score _____

Word Order in Sentences

[Teacher: This activity is about sentences. Listen to the sentence I read. If it is a sentence that makes sense, draw a line under the first answer, "yes." Draw a line under the second answer if the sentence does not make sense. The second answer is "no."]

[Teacher: The flower is pretty.]

1. The flower is pretty.   <u>yes</u>   no

[Teacher: The book is on the table.]

2. The book is on the table.   <u>yes</u>   no

[Teacher: My tall is sister.]

3. My tall is sister.   yes   <u>no</u>

[Teacher: This coat is warm.]

4. This coat is warm.   <u>yes</u>   no

[Teacher: Cat where your is?]

5. Cat where your is?   yes   <u>no</u>

UNIT 2 Shadows • **Lesson 15**

High-Frequency Words

[Teacher: This activity is about words you have learned. Look at each group of words and listen to what I say. Draw a line under the word I say.]

[Teacher: The word is *we*. Draw a line under *we*.]

1. he   <u>we</u>   she

[Teacher: The word is *and*. Draw a line under *and*.

2. <u>and</u>   an   is

[Teacher: The word is *she*. Draw a line under *she*.]

3. the   see   <u>she</u>

[Teacher: The word is *have*. Draw a line under *have*.]

4. big   here   <u>have</u>

[Teacher: The word is *big*. Draw a line under *big*.]

5. and   <u>big</u>   he

UNIT 2 Shadows • **Lesson 16**

Word Length

[**Teacher:** This activity is about words. Look at each group of words. Draw a line under the longest word in each group.]

1. a   if   <u>was</u>

2. <u>with</u>   to   the

3. are   <u>have</u>   on

4. she   in   <u>that</u>

5. is   <u>they</u>   can

LESSON ASSESSMENT

UNIT 2 Shadows • **Lesson 17**

Vocabulary

[Teacher: This activity is about words we learned before. Listen carefully to what I say. Draw a line under the answer you think is right.]

[Teacher: Look at the pictures. Which picture shows someone short...someone short?]

1.

[Teacher: Look at the pictures. Which picture shows a moose...a moose?]

2.

[Teacher: Look at the pictures. Which picture shows someone who is probably puffing...probably puffing?]

3.

[Teacher: Look at the pictures. Which picture shows a person's heel...a person's heel?]

4.
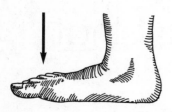  

[Teacher: Look at the pictures. Which picture shows someone doing a jig...doing a jig?]

5.

Vocabulary • Unit 2 Assessment

UNIT 2 **Shadows • Lesson 18**

Fantasy and Reality

[Teacher: This activity is about things that are real and not real. Listen carefully to what I say. Draw a line under the picture that is the best answer to the question I ask.]

[Teacher: Which picture shows fantasy, something that <u>can't</u> happen in real life? Draw a line under something that can't happen in real life.]

1.

[Teacher: Which picture shows fantasy, something that <u>can't</u> happen in real life? Draw a line under something that can't happen in real life.]

2.

[Teacher: Which picture shows fantasy, something that <u>can't</u> happen in real life? Draw a line under something that can't happen in real life.]

3.

[Teacher: Listen carefully. This question is a little different. Which picture shows reality, something that <u>can</u> happen in real life? Draw a line under something that can happen in real life.]

4.

[Teacher: Which picture shows reality, something that <u>can</u> happen in real life? Draw a line under something that can happen in real life.]

5.

Letter Recognition

Directions for the Teacher

Pages 29 and 30 should be used to assess students' knowledge of capital and small letter names for M through Z. This assessment is intended to be administered to students individually.

Duplicate page 29 (capital letters) or 30 (small letters) in the student workbook. Write the student's name and the date on the duplicated page. You will record the student's responses on this page.

Sit beside the student at a table that allows you and the student to work comfortably. Have the student turn to page 29 or 30 in the student workbook; provide whatever help is necessary to ensure that the student is working on the correct page. **Do not have the student mark in the book.** This will allow you to re-administer the assessment, if necessary.

Point to a letter at random and ask the student to name that letter. Avoid pointing to the letters in alphabetical order. You should use a prompt such as "What letter is this?" or "What is the name of this letter?".

Continue the assessment as long as the student seems engaged. If possible, give the student an opportunity to respond to all the letters. Discontinue the assessment if the student is distracted, is responding randomly, or makes five errors in a row.

Letter Recognition *(continued)*

Use the following scoring conventions:

- Use the duplicated page to record the students' responses.
- If the student names the letter correctly on the first try, circle that letter.
- If the student names the letter incorrectly, draw an X over the letter.
- If the student makes an error then self-corrects, put a small question mark beside the letter. Retest the student on this letter after you have tested at least one other letter. You may use the same procedure if a student hesitates for a long time before responding or appears unsure about a letter.
- Do not allow the students to see how you have recorded their responses. Moreover, do not give them feedback about answers being right or wrong.

- After you have tested all the letters and retested those for which the student provided an uncertain response, record the number right, the number wrong, and the number that remain uncertain in the spaces below and on the STUDENT ASSESSMENT RECORD and CLASS ASSESSMENT RECORD. Place the completed page in the student's *cumulative folder*. If any students do not meet the recommended performance level, repeat the assessment after intervention or additional instruction.

UNIT 2 Shadows

Capital Letters

N   U   Q

R   X   T

W   M   O

Z   V   Y

P   S

Number Right: ____

Number Wrong: ____

Number Uncertain: ____

UNIT 2 Shadows

Small Letters

u   o   r

m   x   z

w   v   n

p   y   t

s   q

Number Right: _____

Number Wrong: _____

Number Uncertain: _____

END OF UNIT ASSESSMENT

Alphabet Sequence Part 2

Page 31 should be used to assess students' knowledge of the alphabet sequence. This assessment is intended to be administered individually. Duplicate page 31 in the student workbook and fill in the student's name and the date.

Sit at a table that allows you and the student to work comfortably. You may find it easier to sit beside the student. Have the student turn to page 31 in the student workbook. **Do not have the student mark in the book.** This will allow you to re-administer the assessment, if necessary.

Teacher directions: **This page has some of the letters of the alphabet. Some of the letters are missing. I would like you to say the missing letters of the alphabet in the right order. Let's do the first row together. The two letters are *m* and *n*. What letter comes next in the alphabet? The letter *o* comes next, so I will write the letter *o* in the space. Do you understand what you are supposed to do? Now, I will read the rest of the letters. Tell me the missing letters in the order they appear in the alphabet. If you think about the alphabet song, it will help you.**

After you have completed the assessment, record the number right in the spaces below the columns and on the STUDENT ASSESSMENT RECORD and CLASS ASSESSMENT RECORD. Place the completed page in the student's *cumulative folder*. If any students do not meet the recommended performance level, repeat the assessment after intervention or additional instruction.

UNIT 2 Shadows

Alphabet Sequence

m   n   <u>o</u>

<u>p</u>   q   <u>r</u>

<u>s</u>   <u>t</u>   u

v   <u>w</u>   <u>x</u>

y   <u>z</u>

Alphabet Sequence total: _____

END OF UNIT ASSESSMENT

UNIT 2 Shadows

Matching Capital and Small Letters

[**Teacher:** Some of the letters on this page are missing. I would like you to fill in the missing letters. Sometimes the letters will be capital letters, and sometimes they will be small letters.]

A _a_   B b   C c   D _d_

E e   F f   G _g_   H h

I i   J J   K _k_   L l

M _m_   N n   O o   P P

Q q   R r   S s   T t

U _u_   V v   W w   X x

Y y   Z z

Matching Capital and Small Letters total: _____

UNIT 2 **Shadows**

Action Words

[Teacher: This activity is about verbs, words that show action. Look at each group of pictures carefully. Draw a line under the picture in each group that shows an action, not just a thing.]

1.

2.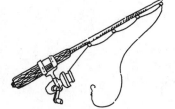

3.

4.

5.

END OF UNIT ASSESSMENT

UNIT 2 Shadows

End Punctuation Marks

[Teacher: This activity is about end marks, the punctuation at the end of a sentence. Listen to the question. Draw a line under the answer you think is right.]

[Teacher: Which of these is a period...a period?]

1. ?   .

[Teacher: Which of these is a question mark...a question mark?]

2. ?   .

[Teacher: Which end mark should go at the end of this sentence? What time is it?]

3. What time is it   ?   .

[Teacher: Which end mark should go at the end of this sentence? I lost my hat.]

4. I lost my hat   ?   .

[Teacher: Which end mark should go at the end of this sentence? The dog is black.]

5. The dog is black   ?   .

[Teacher: Which end mark should go at the end of this sentence? Do you know my teacher?]

6. Do you know my teacher   ?   .

End Punctuation Marks • Unit 2 Assessment

END OF UNIT ASSESSMENT

Introduction

Teacher Directions

The content of this unit consists primarily of skills that immediately precede reading. The assessments and their administration methods are shown below:

Assessment	Method	Recommended Performance Level
Blending Word Parts	Group	4/5
Sentence Boundaries	Group	5/7
Compound Words	Group	4/5
High-Frequency Words	Group	4/5
Setting	Group	4/5
Deleting Syllables	Individual	4/6
Compare and Contrast	Group	4/5
Blending Initial Sounds	Group	4/5
Vocabulary	Group	4/5
Words That Describe	Group	4/5

Although all the assessments relate to the lessons in the unit, the following assessments are the most critical and should be administered to every student. In addition, these are the assessments that the teacher should re-administer if a student does not reach the recommended performance level.

Blending Word Parts
High-Frequency Words
Deleting Syllables
Blending Initial Sounds

UNIT 3 Finding Friends • **Lesson 5**

Blending Word Parts

[Teacher: This activity is about blending word parts. Listen carefully to what I say. Draw a line under the picture whose name I say.]

[Teacher: Build   ing. Draw a line under the build   ing.]

1.

[Teacher: Per   son. Draw a line under the per   son.]

2.

[Teacher: Flow   er. Draw a line under the flow   er.]

3.

[Teacher: News   paper. Draw a line under the news   paper.]

4.

[Teacher: Fac   tory. Draw a line under the fac   tory.]

5.

Name _____ Date _____ Score _____

Sentence Boundaries

[**Teacher:** Listen while I read this paragraph. When I am finished, draw a line under the first and last word of each sentence.]

Jane walks to school with Tom. They

are friends. They live on the same street.

Jane and Tom have pets. Jane has a cat.

Tom has a dog. Even their pets are friends.

Beginning words total: _____

Ending words total: _____

UNIT 3 **Finding Friends • Lesson 7**

Compound Words

[Teacher: This activity is about compound words. A compound word is made up of two smaller words. Catfish is a compound word. It is made up of cat and fish. Listen to the word I say. The word is in the box. Draw a line under the first answer if the word is a compound word. The first answer is "yes." Draw a line under the second answer if the word I say is not a compound word. The second answer is "no."]

[Teacher: The word is *sidewalk*. Is this a compound word? Draw a line under yes or no.]

1. | sidewalk | yes   no

[Teacher: The word is *animal*. Is this a compound word? Draw a line under yes or no.]

2. | animal | yes   no

[Teacher: The word is *baseball*. Is this a compound word? Draw a line under yes or no.]

3. | baseball | yes   no

[Teacher: The word is *children*. Is this a compound word? Draw a line under yes or no.]

4. | children | yes   no

[Teacher: The word is *something*. Is this a compound word? Draw a line under yes or no.]

5. | something | yes   no

UNIT 3   **Finding Friends • Lesson 15**

High-Frequency Words

[Teacher: This activity is about words you have learned. Look at each group of words and listen to what I say. Draw a line under the word I say.]

[Teacher: The word is *go*. Draw a line under *go*.]

1.   <u>go</u>   big   grow

[Teacher: The word is *up*. Draw a line under *up*.]

2.   the   <u>up</u>   and

[Teacher: The word is *do*. Draw a line under *do*.]

3.   has   down   <u>do</u>

[Teacher: The word is *who*. Draw a line under *who*.]

4.   <u>who</u>   we   have

[Teacher: The word is *are*. Draw a line under *are*.]

5.   and   <u>are</u>   the

LESSON ASSESSMENT

UNIT 3   **Finding Friends • Lesson 16**

Setting

[Teacher: This activity is about setting, where stories take place. Listen to each story I read. Draw a line under the picture that shows where the story takes place.]

[Teacher: Matthew likes to read. He and his mother often go to the library where there are lots of books.]

1.
  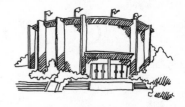

[Teacher: The squirrel heard the big dog coming down the forest trail. Quickly, the squirrel ran up the tree where it would be safe.]

2.
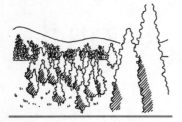  

[Teacher: Laura sat on the steps and looked up the street. Her friend, Beth, was coming over to go roller-blading.]

3.

[Teacher: The family of goats lived high in the mountains. They felt safe among the steep slopes and rocky cliffs.]

4.

[Teacher: Riesa and her family lived on a farm. They had lots of animals, and Riesa even had her own horse.]

5.

Deleting Syllables

Teacher Directions

This assessment is intended to be administered to students individually. Duplicate this page for each student you choose to assess. Write the student's name and today's date in the appropriate spaces. You will record the student's responses on this page.

Sit at a table that allows you and the student to work comfortably. You may find it easier to sit across from the student rather than beside the student.

Teacher: I am going to say a word. Then I am going to say it again, but one part of the word will be missing. I want you to tell me the missing part. Here's a practice word: catfish...cat. What part of the word is missing? catfish...cat

You may repeat the practice activity using the word *football* if you are not sure the student understands what to do. When the student is ready, say each complete word and then part of the word on page 40B. Check the box beside each word that the student completes correctly.

After you have completed the assessment, record the number right in the space below the words and on the STUDENT ASSESSMENT RECORD and CLASS ASSESSMENT RECORD. Place the completed page in the student's *cumulative folder*. If any students do not reach the recommended performance level, repeat the assessment after intervention or additional instruction.

LESSON ASSESSMENT

UNIT 3 Finding Friends • **Lesson 17**

Deleting Syllables

outside…out   side   ☐

fireplace…fire   place   ☐

doorway…door   way   ☐

bedroom…room   bed   ☐

highway…way   high   ☐

raincoat…coat   rain   ☐

Deleting Syllables total: _____

UNIT 3   Finding Friends • **Lesson 18**

Compare and Contrast

[**Teacher:** Look at the picture in the box and the other pictures while you listen to what I say. Draw a line under the answer you think is right.]

[**Teacher:** The picture in the box is a bird. Draw a line under the other picture of something that is like the bird because it can fly.]

1.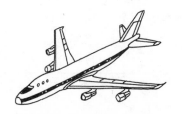

[**Teacher:** The picture in the box is a tomato. Draw a line under the other picture of something that is like the tomato because you can eat it.]

2.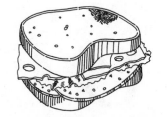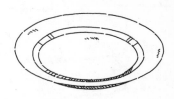

[**Teacher:** The picture in the box is a book. Draw a line under the other picture of something that is like the book because you can read it.]

3.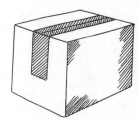

[**Teacher:** Listen carefully. This one is a little different. The picture in the box is a car. Draw a line under the other picture of something that is different from the car because you can't ride in it.]

4.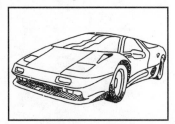

[**Teacher:** The picture in the box is a house. Draw a line under the other picture of something that is different from the house because you can't go inside it.]

5.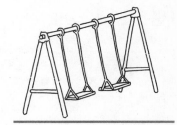

UNIT 3 Finding Friends • **Lesson 19**

Blending Initial Sounds

[**Teacher:** This activity is about blending sounds to make words. Listen carefully to what I say. Draw a line under the picture whose name I say.]

[**Teacher:** F   ish. Draw a line under the f   ish.]

1.

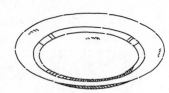  

[**Teacher:** B   ook. Draw a line under the b   ook.]

2.

[**Teacher:** m   op. Draw a line under the m   op.]

3.

[**Teacher:** D   esk. Draw a line under the d   esk.]

4.

[**Teacher:** C   at. Draw a line under the c   at.]

5.

UNIT 3 Finding Friends

Vocabulary

[Teacher: This activity is about words we learned before. Listen carefully to what I say. Draw a line under the answer you think is right.]

[Teacher: Look at the pictures. Which picture shows something delicious...something delicious?]

1.

[Teacher: Look at the pictures. Which picture shows someone happy...someone happy?]

2.

[Teacher: Look at the pictures. Which picture shows something that has burst...something that has burst?]

3.

[Teacher: Look at the pictures. Which picture shows a winter scene...a winter scene?]

4.

[Teacher: Look at the pictures. Which picture shows an animal scampering...an animal scampering?]

5.

UNIT 3   **Finding Friends**

Words That Describe

[Teacher: This activity is about words that describe. Listen to the word I say. The word is in the box. Draw a line under the first answer if the word describes. The first answer is "yes." Draw a line under the second answer if the word I say does not describe. The second answer is "no."]

[Teacher: The word is *cold*. Is this a word that describes? Draw a line under yes or no.]

1.    yes   no

[Teacher: The word is *two*. Is this a word that describes? Draw a line under yes or no.]

2.   yes   no

[Teacher: The word is *door*. Is this a word that describes? Draw a line under yes or no.]

3. 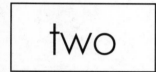   yes   no

[Teacher: The word is *red*. Is this a word that describes? Draw a line under yes or no.]

4.    yes   no

[Teacher: The word is *car*. Is this a word that describes? Draw a line under yes or no.]

5.   yes   no

Words That Describe • Unit 3 Assessment

END OF UNIT ASSESSMENT

Introduction

Teacher Directions

The content of this unit consists of a variety of skills, including the association of letter shapes and sounds. The assessments and their administration methods are shown below:

Assessment	Method	Recommended Performance Level
Days of the Week	Group	4/5
Following Directions	Group	3/5
Letter Sounds (s, d, p, m)	Group	4/6
High-Frequency Words	Group	4/5
Vocabulary	Group	4/5
Plot	Group	4/5
Word Pairs	Group	5/5
Letter Sounds (h, s, d, p, m, t, n)	Group	4/6
Long Vowel Sounds	Group	5/5
Words That Describe	Group	4/5

Although all the assessments relate to the lessons in the unit, the following assessments are the most critical and should be administered to every student. In addition, these are the assessments that the teacher should re-administer if a student does not reach the recommended performance level.

High-Frequency Words
Letter Sounds
Word Pairs
Long Vowel Sounds

UNIT 4   The Wind • **Lesson 2**

Days of the Week

[Teacher: This activity is about days of the week. Listen carefully to what I say. Draw a line under the word that is a day of the week.]

[Teacher: The answers are Monday, Year, Minute. Which one is a day of the week? Monday, Year, Minute]

1. <u>Monday</u>   Year   Minute

[Teacher: The answers are Vacation, Surprise, Saturday. Which one is a day of the week? Vacation, Surprise, Saturday]

2. Vacation   Surprise   <u>Saturday</u>

[Teacher: The answers are Wonderful, Wednesday, Week. Which one is a day of the week? Wonderful, Wednesday, Week]

3. Wonderful   <u>Wednesday</u>   Week

[Teacher: The answers are Friday, Friendly, Snowy. Which one is a day of the week? Friday, Friendly, Snowy]

4. <u>Friday</u>   Friendly   Snowy

[Teacher: The answers are Somewhere, Sunday, Shadow. Which one is a day of the week? Somewhere, Sunday, Shadow]

5. Somewhere   <u>Sunday</u>   Shadow

UNIT 4 The Wind • **Lesson 5**

Following Directions

[Teacher: Listen carefully to the directions I say. Draw a line under the picture that shows what the directions say to do.]

[Teacher: Mrs. Begay asked Cindy to go to the kitchen, get a glass of water, and bring it to Grandmother.]

1.

[Teacher: Mark's teacher asked him to go to the library, borrow a book about dinosaurs, and put it on her desk.]

2.

[Teacher: Dad asked Ryan to pick up his baseball glove, put it in the closet in his room, and close the door.]

3.

[Teacher: Lisa asked her mother to hammer a nail in her wall and hang a picture for her.]

4.

[Teacher: Uncle Jeff asked Dennis to get the leash and take the dog outside for a walk.]

5.

UNIT 4 The Wind • **Lesson 10**

Letter Sounds (s, d, p, m)

[Teacher: This activity is about letter sounds. Listen carefully to what I say. Draw a line under the letter you think is right.]

[Teacher: The word in the box is *mat*. Which letter should go at the beginning of the word *mat?*]

1. | __at | b   m   f

[Teacher: The word in the box is *sit*. Which letter should go at the beginning of the word *sit?*]

2. | __it | s   b   p

[Teacher: The word in the box is *pot*. Which letter should go at the beginning of the word *pot?*]

3. | __ot | d   r   p

[Teacher: The word in the box is *map*. Which letter should go at the end of the word *map?*]

4. | ma__ | p   t   n

[Teacher: The word in the box is *him*. Which letter should go at the end of the word *him?*]

5. | hi__ | d   m   t

[Teacher: The word in the box is *mud*. Which letter should go at the end of the word *mud?*]

6. | mu__ | t   g   d

UNIT 4 The Wind • **Lesson 15**

High-Frequency Words

[Teacher: This activity is about words you have learned. Look at each group of words and listen to what I say. Draw a line under the word I say.]

[Teacher: The word is *what*. Draw a line under *what*.]

1. you   <u>what</u>   we

[Teacher: The word is *can*. Draw a line under *can*.]

2. <u>can</u>   do   cat

[Teacher: The word is *you*. Draw a line under *you*.]

3. yes   who   <u>you</u>

[Teacher: The word is *at*. Draw a line under *at*.]

4. are   <u>at</u>   is

[Teacher: The word is *like*. Draw a line under *like*.]

5. you   too   <u>like</u>

UNIT 4 The Wind • **Lesson 17**

Vocabulary

[Teacher: This activity is about words we learned before. Listen carefully to what I say. Draw a line under the answer you think is right.]

[Teacher: Look at the pictures. Which picture shows a meadow...a meadow?]

1.

[Teacher: Look at the pictures. Which picture shows a fierce animal...a fierce animal?]

2.

[Teacher: Look at the pictures. Which picture shows a person tossing something...a person tossing something?]

3.

[Teacher: Look at the pictures. Which picture shows a horse being brushed...a horse being brushed?]

4.

[Teacher: Look at the pictures. Which picture shows a person strumming...a person strumming?]

5.

Vocabulary • **Unit 4 Assessment**

Name _____ Date _____ Score _____

UNIT 4   The Wind • **Lesson 19**

Plot

[**Teacher:** Listen to what I say. Draw a line under the answer you think is right.]

[**Teacher:** A big storm blew the ship onto the island. The people climbed onto the beach. They wondered what they would do now. Which picture shows what this story is about?]

1.

[**Teacher:** Karen was so excited. Her mother was coming home from the hospital today. Karen had a new baby brother. Which picture shows what this story is about?]

2.

[**Teacher:** Reggie carried the groceries from the car to the kitchen. Karen and their mother put them away. Which picture shows what this story is about?]

3.

[**Teacher:** The empty lot was filled with trash. It wasn't very pretty. Some people decided to solve the problem. Which picture shows the best way to solve the problem?]

4.

[**Teacher:** The snow was so deep that school was closed. The children had a wonderful time playing outside. Which picture shows what the children were doing?]

5.

Unit 4 Assessment • *Plot*

UNIT 4 The Wind

Word Pairs

[Teacher: Listen to the words I say. If they are the same, draw a line under the first word. The word is "yes." If the words are different, draw a line under the second word. The word is "no."]

[Teacher: The words are <u>run</u> and <u>run</u>. Draw a line under the first word if they are the same or the second word if they are different...<u>run</u> and <u>run</u>.]

1.   <u>yes</u>   no

[Teacher: The words are <u>call</u> and <u>tall</u>. Draw a line under the first word if they are the same or the second word if they are different...<u>call</u> and <u>tall</u>.]

2.   yes   <u>no</u>

[Teacher: The words are <u>bed</u> and <u>bed</u>. Draw a line under the first word if they are the same or the second word if they are different...<u>bed</u> and <u>bed</u>.]

3.   <u>yes</u>   no

[Teacher: The words are <u>made</u> and <u>paid</u>. Draw a line under the first word if they are the same or the second word if they are different...<u>made</u> and <u>paid</u>.]

4.   yes   <u>no</u>

[Teacher: The words are <u>men</u> and <u>mean</u>. Draw a line under the first word if they are the same or the second word if they are different...<u>men</u> and <u>mean</u>.]

5.   yes   <u>no</u>

END OF UNIT ASSESSMENT

UNIT 4 The Wind

Letter Sounds (h, s, d, p, m, t, n)

[Teacher: This activity is about letter sounds. Listen carefully to what I say. Draw a line under the letter you think is right.]

[Teacher: The word in the box is *not*. Which letter should go at the beginning of the word *not*?]

1. | __ot | h   n   p

[Teacher: The word in the box is *his*. Which letter should go at the beginning of the word *his*?]

2. | __is | s   n   h

[Teacher: The word in the box is *tin*. Which letter should go at the beginning of the word *tin*?]

3. | __in | t   f   p

[Teacher: The word in the box is *sad*. Which letter should go at the end of the word *sad*?]

4. | sa__ | p   t   d

[Teacher: The word in the box is *man*. Which letter should go at the end of the word *man*?]

5. | ma__ | n   t   d

[Teacher: The word in the box is *sun*. Which letter should go at the beginning of the word *sun*?]

6. | __un | f   r   s

END OF UNIT ASSESSMENT

UNIT 4 The Wind

Long Vowel Sounds

[Teacher: This activity is about letter sounds. Listen carefully to what I say. Draw a line under the letter you think is right.]

[Teacher: Which letter do you hear in the middle of the word late...late?]

1.   e   <u>a</u>   i

[Teacher: Which letter do you hear in the middle of the word meet...meet?]

2.   o   u   <u>e</u>

[Teacher: Which letter do you hear in the middle of the word bike...bike?]

3.   <u>i</u>   e   a

[Teacher: Which letter do you hear in the middle of the word hope...hope?]

4.   a   u   <u>o</u>

[Teacher: Which letter do you hear in the middle of the word cute...cute?]

5.   e   <u>u</u>   i

END OF UNIT ASSESSMENT

UNIT 4   **The Wind**

Words That Describe

[Teacher: This activity is about words that describe. Listen to the word I say. The word is in the box. Draw a line under the first answer if the word describes. The first answer is "yes." Draw a line under the second answer if the word I say does not describe. The second answer is "no."]

[Teacher: The word is *horse*. Is this a word that describes? Draw a line under yes or no.]

1. | horse | yes   <u>no</u>

[Teacher: The word is *quiet*. Is this a word that describes? Draw a line under yes or no.]

2. | quiet | <u>yes</u>   no

[Teacher: The word is *under*. Is this a word that describes? Draw a line under yes or no.]

3. | under | <u>yes</u>   no

[Teacher: The word is *crayon*. Is this a word that describes? Draw a line under yes or no.]

4. | crayon | yes   <u>no</u>

[Teacher: The word is *soft*. Is this a word that describes? Draw a line under yes or no.]

5. | soft | <u>yes</u>   no

Introduction

Teacher Directions

The content of this unit consists of a variety of skills, including the association of letter shapes and sounds. In addition, students receive more intense instruction in the location of sounds in words. The assessments and their administration methods are shown below:

Assessment	Method	Recommended Performance Level
Beginning and Ending Sounds	Group	6/6
Predicting	Group	3/5
Listening for Problems	Group	4/5
High-Frequency Words	Group	4/5
Quotation Marks	Group	3/5
Vocabulary	Group	4/5
Letter Sounds		
(Ll, short a, short i)	Group	4/6
Sounds in Words	Group	5/5
Words That Show Action	Group	3/5

Although all the assessments relate to the lessons in the unit, the following assessments are the most critical and should be administered to every student. In addition, these are the assessments that the teacher should re-administer if a student does not reach the recommended performance level.

Beginning and Ending Sounds
High-Frequency Words
Letter Sounds (l, short a, short i)
Sounds in Words

UNIT 5 **Stick to It • Lesson 5**

Beginning and Ending Sounds

[Teacher: This activity is about beginning and ending sounds. Listen carefully to what I say. Draw a line under the answer you think is right.]

[Teacher: Which word begins with a different sound? The answers are sit, sun, ran.]

1.

sit   sun   ran

[Teacher: Which word begins with a different sound? The answers are get, man, mud.]

2.

get   man   mud

[Teacher: Which word begins with a different sound? The answers are win, van, wet.]

3.

win   van   wet

[Teacher: This one is a little different. Which word ends with a different sound? The answers are mad, cab, bib.]

4.

mad   cab   bib

[Teacher: Which word ends with a different sound? The answers are fat, bit, rub.]

5.

fat   bit   rub

[Teacher: Which word ends with a different sound? The answers are win, wet, van.]

6.

win   wet   van

Unit 5 Assessment • *Beginning and Ending Sounds*   Unit 5 • Lesson 5   **54**

UNIT 5 Stick to It • **Lesson 6**

Predicting

[Teacher: This activity is about making predictions. Listen carefully to what I say. Draw a line under the answer you think is right.]

[Teacher: Tina is wearing lots of clothes because it is cold outside. Which picture shows what Tina will probably do outside?]

1.

[Teacher: Kim is hungry. Which picture shows what she will probably do next?]

2.

[Teacher: It is fall. Pete is helping his mother outside. What is Pete probably doing?]

3.

[Teacher: The Blake family is going someplace where they will see a lot of animals. Where do you think they will go?]

4.

[Teacher: The car ran over a nail in the road. Which picture shows what will happen next?]

5.

UNIT 5   Stick to It • **Lesson 9**

Listening for Problems

[Teacher: Listen to what I say. Draw a line under the answer you think is right.]

[Teacher: Nancy was sick. She was sad because she couldn't go to the football game. Her friends went without her. What is the problem in this story?]

1.

[Teacher: Some children were playing baseball. One of them hit the ball on the roof. Now the children can't play baseball. What is the problem in this story?]

2.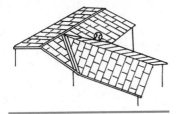

[Teacher: The Gonzales family was going to the movies. Mr. Gonzales noticed that the car had a flat tire. What is the problem in this story?]

3.

[Teacher: The parade was wonderful. There was only one thing wrong. Jeff couldn't see because of the people in front of him. What is the problem in this story?]

4.

[Teacher: Bart was flying his kite. The string broke and the kite blew away. What is the problem in this story?]

5.

UNIT 5 Stick to It • **Lesson 14**

High-Frequency Words

[Teacher: This activity is about words you have learned. Look at each group of words and listen to what I say. Draw a line under the word I say.]

[Teacher: The word is *on*. Draw a line under *on*.]

1.

and   on   an

[Teacher: The word is *has*. Draw a line under *has*.]

2.

has   have   here

[Teacher: The word is *not*. Draw a line under *not*.]

3.

no   on   not

[Teacher: The word is *at*. Draw a line under *at*.]

4.

can   at   an

[Teacher: The word is *do*. Draw a line under *do*.]

5.

no   you   do

UNIT 5 **Stick to It • Lesson 16**

Quotation Marks

[Teacher: This activity is about dialogue and quotation marks. I will read a sentence. The sentence is printed on the page. Draw a line under the first answer if the sentence needs quotation marks because someone is speaking. The first answer is "yes." Draw a line under the second answer if the sentence does not need quotation marks. The second answer is "no."]

[Teacher: Mom said, Dinner is ready. Does this sentence need quotation marks? Draw a line under yes or no.]

1. Mom said, Dinner is ready.   yes   no

[Teacher: Where is the cat? asked Mark. Does this sentence need quotation marks? Draw a line under yes or no.]

2. Where is the cat? asked Mark.   yes   no

[Teacher: It is time to go to bed. Does this sentence need quotation marks? Draw a line under yes or no.]

3. It is time to go to bed.   yes   no

[Teacher: Helen said, Let's play ball. Does this sentence need quotation marks? Draw a line under yes or no.]

4. Helen said, Let's play ball.   yes   no

[Teacher: The snow is deep. Does this sentence need quotation marks? Draw a line under yes or no.]

5. The snow is deep.   yes   no

LESSON ASSESSMENT

UNIT 5 Stick to It • **Lesson 18**

Vocabulary

[Teacher: This activity is about words we learned before. Listen carefully to what I say. Draw a line under the answer you think is right.]

[Teacher: Look at the pictures. Which picture shows something enormous...something enormous?]

1.

[Teacher: Look at the pictures. Which picture shows someone chatting...someone chatting?]

2.

[Teacher: Look at the pictures. Which picture shows confetti...confetti?]

3.

[Teacher: Look at the pictures. Which picture shows a bloom...a bloom?]

4.

[Teacher: Look at the pictures. Which picture shows an invitation...an invitation?]

5.

UNIT 5 Stick to It • **Lesson 19**

Letter Sounds (Ll, short a, short i)

[Teacher: This activity is about letter sounds. Listen carefully to what I say. Draw a line under the letter you think is right.]

[Teacher: The word in the box is *let*. Which letter should go at the beginning of the word *let*?]

1. 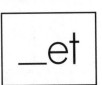   l̲   b   m

[Teacher: The word in the box is *hat*. Which letter should go in the middle of the word *hat*?]

2. 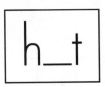   e   i   a̲

[Teacher: The word in the box is *hid*. Which letter should go in the middle of the word *hid*?]

3. 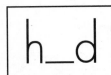   u   i̲   o

[Teacher: The word in the box is *lap*. Which letter should go at the beginning of the word *lap*?]

4. 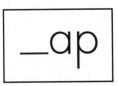   c   l̲   m

[Teacher: The word in the box is *bit*. Which letter should go in the middle of the word *bit*?]

5.   u   e   i̲

[Teacher: The word in the box is *ran*. Which letter should go in the middle of the word *ran*?]

6. 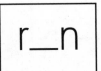   a̲   o   e

UNIT 5 Stick to It

Sounds in Words

[Teacher: This activity is about where you hear sounds in words. Listen carefully to the sound I say and the word. Draw a line under the answer that tells where the sound is in the word. The answers are Beginning, Middle, End.]

[Teacher: The word is bat. Where do you hear the b sound? Is it in the beginning, middle, or end? Where is the b in bat?]

1.
Beginning   Middle   End

[Teacher: The word is seem. Where do you hear the e sound? Is it in the beginning, middle, or end? Where is the e in seem?]

2.
Beginning   Middle   End

[Teacher: The word is red. Where do you hear the d sound? Is it in the beginning, middle, or end? Where is the d in red?]

3.
Beginning   Middle   End

[Teacher: The word is boat. Where do you hear the o sound? Is it in the beginning, middle, or end? Where is the o in boat?]

4.
Beginning   Middle   End

[Teacher: The word is net. Where do you hear the n sound? Is it in the beginning, middle, or end? Where is the n in net?]

5.
Beginning   Middle   End

END OF UNIT ASSESSMENT

UNIT 5 Stick to It

Words That Show Action

[Teacher: This activity is about words that show action and present, past, and future tenses. Listen carefully to what I say.]

[Teacher: Mary swims at the beach. Draw a line under the word that shows action.]

1.

Mary swims at the beach.

[Teacher: Tim reads at the library. Draw a line under the word that shows action.]

2.

Tim reads at the library.

[Teacher: The dog runs. Is this something in the past, present, or future? Draw a line under the answer you think is right.]

3.

Past   Present   Future

[Teacher: My sister was born last year. Is this something in the past, present, or future? Draw a line under the answer you think is right.]

4.

Past   Present   Future

[Teacher: Next summer, we will go to the beach. Is this something in the past, present, or future? Draw a line under the answer you think is right.]

5.

Past   Present   Future

Introduction

Teacher Directions

The content of this unit consists of a variety of skills, including the association of letter shapes and sounds. In addition, students receive more intense instruction in the location of sounds in words. The assessments and their administration methods are shown below:

Assessment	Method	Recommended Performance Level
Main Idea	Group	3/5
Phoneme Replacement	Group	3/5
Letter Sounds (n, d, b, c)	Group	4/6
Vocabulary	Group	4/5
Letter Sounds (r, g, j)	Group	4/5
High-Frequency Words	Group	4/5
Capital Letters and End Marks	Group	3/5

Although all the assessments relate to the lessons in the unit, the following assessments are the most critical and should be administered to every student. In addition, these are the assessments that the teacher should readminister if a student does not reach the recommended performance level.

Letter Sounds (n, d, b, c)
Letter Sounds (r, g, j)
High-Frequency Words

UNIT 6 Red, White, and Blue • **Lesson 4**

Main Idea

[**Teacher:** This activity is about main idea. Listen to each story. Draw a line under the picture that best shows what the story tells.]

[**Teacher:** Wendy is standing on the diving board. She is getting ready to dive into the water. Draw a line under the picture that matches this story.]

1.

[**Teacher:** Duane is raking leaves on his lawn. When he is finished, he will clean his room. Draw a line under the picture that matches this story.]

2.

[**Teacher:** The Miller family was eating dinner. Their dog was under the table. Draw a line under the picture that matches this story.]

3.

[**Teacher:** The school bus parked in front of the school. The children were getting off the bus. Draw a line under the picture that matches this story.]

4.

[**Teacher:** Mrs. Powell sat on her porch. Patrick walked by and said hello. Draw a line under the picture that matches this story.]

5.

UNIT 6 Red, White, and Blue • **Lesson 6**

Phoneme Replacement

[**Teacher:** This activity is about making new words. Look at each group of pictures and listen to what I say. Draw a line under the answer you think is right.]

[**Teacher:** Listen to this word: /s/ /un/. If you take away the /s/ and change the first sound to /r/, what new word did you make?]

1.

[**Teacher:** Listen to this word: /l/ /ike/. If you take away the /l/ and change the first sound to /b/, what new word did you make?]

2.

[**Teacher:** Listen to this word: /n/ /eed/. If you take away the /n/ and change the first sound to /r/, what new word did you make?]

3.

[**Teacher:** Listen to this word: /b/ /ake/. If you take away the /b/ and change the first sound to /l/, what new word did you make?]

4.

[**Teacher:** Listen to this word: /h/ /ouse/. If you take away the /h/ and change the first sound to /m/, what new word did you make?]

5.

Phoneme Replacement • Unit 6 Assessment

UNIT 6 Red, White, and Blue • **Lesson II**

Letter Sounds (n, d, b, c)

[Teacher: This activity is about letter sounds. Listen carefully to what I say. Draw a line under the letter you think is right.]

[Teacher: The word in the box is *not*. Which letter should go at the beginning of the word *not*?]

1.
  _ot   <u>n</u>   d   h

[Teacher: The word in the box is *dig*. Which letter should go at the beginning of the word *dig*?]

2.
  _ig   b   f   <u>d</u>

[Teacher: The word in the box is *can*. Which letter should go at the beginning of the word *can*?]

3.
  _an   m   <u>c</u>   r

[Teacher: The word in the box is *cab*. Which letter should go at the end of the word *cab*?]

4.
  ca_   r   n   <u>b</u>

[Teacher: The word in the box is *fun*. Which letter should go at the end of the word *fun*?]

5.
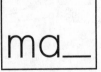 fu_   <u>n</u>   r   s

[Teacher: The word in the box is *mad*. Which letter should go at the end of the word *mad*?]

6.
    ma_   r   <u>d</u>   n

LESSON ASSESSMENT

Name _____ Date _____ Score _____

UNIT 6 Red, White, and Blue • Lesson 17

Vocabulary

[Teacher: This activity is about words we learned before. Listen carefully to what I say. Draw a line under the answer you think is right.]

[Teacher: Look at the pictures. Which picture shows a country...a country?]

1.

[Teacher: Look at the pictures. Which picture shows an object that can spin...something that can spin?]

2.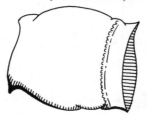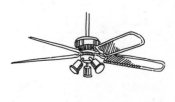

[Teacher: Look at the pictures. Which picture shows someone shouting...someone shouting?]

3.

[Teacher: Look at the pictures. Which picture shows something you might see in a parade...a parade?]

4.

[Teacher: Look at the pictures. Which picture shows a courthouse...a courthouse?]

5.

UNIT 6   Red, White, and Blue • **Lesson 20**

Letter Sounds (r, g, j)

[Teacher: This activity is about letter sounds. Listen carefully to what I say. Draw a line under the letter you think is right.]

[Teacher: The word in the box is *ran*. Which letter should go at the beginning of the word *ran*?]

1.

    t   f   <u>r</u>

[Teacher: The word in the box is *got*. Which letter should go at the beginning of the word *got*?]

2.

    n   <u>g</u>   l

[Teacher: The word in the box is *jar*. Which letter should go at the beginning of the word *jar*?]

3.

    f   t   <u>j</u>

[Teacher: The word in the box is *rug*. Which letter should go at the end of the word *rug*?]

4.

    <u>g</u>   b   n

[Teacher: The word in the box is *car*. Which letter should go at the end of the word *car*?]

5.

    n   <u>r</u>   y

UNIT 6 Red, White, and Blue

High-Frequency Words

[Teacher: This activity is about words you have learned. Look at each group of words and listen to what I say. Draw a line under the word I say.]

[Teacher: The word is *my*. Draw a line under *my*.]

1.   we   <u>my</u>   me

[Teacher: The word is *and*. Draw a line under *and*.]

2.   <u>and</u>   are   an

[Teacher: The word is *this*. Draw a line under *this*.]

3.   the   what   <u>this</u>

[Teacher: The word is *can*. Draw a line under *can*.]

4.   have   <u>can</u>   you

[Teacher: The word is *what*. Draw a line under *what*.]

5.   we   who   <u>what</u>

END OF UNIT ASSESSMENT

Name _____ Date _____ Score _____

UNIT 6 Red, White, and Blue

Capital Letters and End Marks in Sentences

[Teacher: This activity is about capital letters and end marks. I will read a sentence. The sentence is printed on the page. Some of the words are in dark type. Draw a line under the word in each sentence that needs a capital letter. Then, circle the end mark.]

[Teacher: This is my hat. Draw a line under the word in dark type that needs a capital letter. Circle the end mark.]

1. this is **my hat**.

[Teacher: We will visit judy. Draw a line under the word in dark type that needs a capital letter. Circle the end mark.]

2. We **will visit judy**.

[Teacher: Did you play at the park? Draw a line under the word in dark type that needs a capital letter. Circle the end mark.]

3. did you play at the **park**?

[Teacher: You did a great job! Draw a line under the word in dark type that needs a capital letter. Circle the end mark.]

4. you did a **great** job!

[Teacher: Our teacher's name is Mr. Hill. Draw a line under the word in dark type that needs a capital letter. Circle the end mark.]

5. Our teacher's **name is mr.** Hill.

Unit 6 Assessment • *Capital Letters and End Marks in Sentences*

Introduction

Teacher Directions

The content of this unit consists of a variety of skills, including the association of letter shapes and sounds. In addition, students are taught the lower-frequency consonants and the critical /e/ sound. The assessments and their administration methods are shown below:

Assessment	Method	Recommended Performance Level
Counting Phonemes	Group	4/5
Letter Sounds (f, x, z, w, e)	Group	4/6
Vocabulary	Group	4/5
Letter Sounds (k, q, y, v, e)	Group	4/5
Pronouns	Group	4/5

Although all the assessments relate to the lessons in the unit, the following assessments are the most critical and should be administered to every student. In addition, these are the assessments that the teacher should re-administer if a student does not reach the recommended performance level.

Counting Phonemes
Letter Sounds (f, x, z, w, e)
Letter Sounds (k, q, y, v, e)

UNIT 7 Teamwork • **Lesson 5**

Counting Phonemes

[Teacher: This activity is about counting sounds in words. Listen carefully to the word I say. Draw a line under the answer that shows how many sounds are in the word.]

[Teacher: How many sounds are in the word *at*? The answers are two, three, four.]

1.
2   3   4

[Teacher: How many sounds are in the word *run*? The answers are two, three, four.]

2.
2   3   4

[Teacher: How many sounds are in the word *see*? The answers are two, three, four.]

3.
2   3   4

[Teacher: How many sounds are in the word *men*? The answers are two, three, four.]

4.
2   3   4

[Teacher: How many sounds are in the word *desk*? The answers are two, three, four.]

5.
2   3   4

LESSON ASSESSMENT

LESSON ASSESSMENT

UNIT 7 • Teamwork • **Lesson 10**

Letter Sounds (f, x, z, w, e)

[Teacher: This activity is about letter sounds. Listen carefully to what I say. Draw a line under the letter you think is right.]

[Teacher: The word in the box is *far*. Which letter should go at the beginning of the word *far*?]

1.

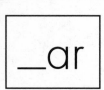 t   c   <u>f</u>

[Teacher: The word in the box is *fox*. Which letter should go at the end of the word *fox*?]

2.

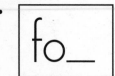 <u>x</u>   r   m

[Teacher: The word in the box is *zoo*. Which letter should go at the beginning of the word *zoo*?]

3.

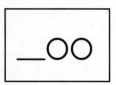 m   <u>z</u>   t

[Teacher: The word in the box is *nose*. Which letter is missing from the word *nose*?]

4.

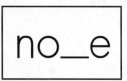 <u>s</u>   t   n

[Teacher: The word in the box is *saw*. Which letter should go at the end of the word *saw*?]

5.

 d   t   <u>w</u>

[Teacher: The word in the box is *met*. Which letter should go in the middle of the word *met*?]

6.

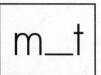 a   <u>e</u>   o

Name _____ Date _____ Score _____

Vocabulary

[**Teacher:** This activity is about words we learned before. Listen carefully to what I say. Draw a line under the answer you think is right.]

[**Teacher:** Look at the pictures. Which picture shows a group...a group?]

1.

[**Teacher:** Look at the pictures. Which picture shows teamwork...teamwork?]

2.
 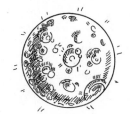 

[**Teacher:** Look at the pictures. Which picture shows creatures...creatures?]

3.

[**Teacher:** Look at the pictures. Which picture shows something you might see during midday...midday?]

4.

[**Teacher:** Look at the pictures. Which picture shows rubbish...rubbish?]

5.

UNIT 7 Teamwork • Lesson 18

Letter Sounds (k, q, y, v, e)

[Teacher: This activity is about letter sounds. Listen carefully to what I say. Draw a line under the letter you think is right.]

[Teacher: The word in the box is *keep*. Which letter should go at the beginning of the word *keep*?]

1.

   b   <u>k</u>   w

[Teacher: The word in the box is *quiet*. Which letter should go at the beginning of the word *quiet*?]

2.

   <u>q</u>   b   s

[Teacher: The word in the box is *yes*. Which letter should go at the beginning of the word *yes*?]

3.

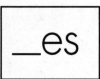   n   d   <u>y</u>

[Teacher: The word in the box is *van*. Which letter should go at the beginning of the word *van*?]

4.

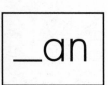   <u>v</u>   t   r

[Teacher: The word in the box is *bed*. Which letter should go in the middle of the word *bed*?]

5.

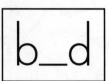   a   <u>e</u>   u

UNIT 7 Teamwork

Pronouns

[Teacher: This activity is about pronouns. Listen carefully to what I say. Draw a line under the answer you think is right.]

[Teacher: Bob went home. Which pronoun can take the place of Bob? The answers are she, he, we.]

1.

she   <u>he</u>   we

[Teacher: Sue is my friend. Which pronoun can take the place of Sue? The answers are she, I, you.]

2.

<u>she</u>   I   you

[Teacher: That is my bike. Which pronoun can take the place of my bike? The answers are we, I, it.]

3.

we   I   <u>it</u>

[Teacher: Mom and I like checkers. Which pronoun can take the place of Mom and I? The answers are she, we, they.]

4.

she   <u>we</u>   they

[Teacher: Juan and Kim are here. Which pronoun can take the place of Juan and Kim? The answers are they, he, she.]

5.

<u>they</u>   he   she

END OF UNIT ASSESSMENT

Introduction

Teacher Directions

This unit reviews critical skills and teaches students more advanced applications of the association of letter shapes and sounds. The assessments and their administration methods are shown below:

Assessment	Method	Recommended Performance Level
Rhyme Mime	Group	4/5
Words in Context	Group	4/5
High-Frequency Words	Group	4/5
Figurative Language	Group	4/5
Word Building	Group	4/5
Long Vowel Review	Group	5/5
Short Vowel Review	Group	5/5

Although all the assessments relate to the lessons in the unit, the following assessments are the most critical and should be administered to every student. In addition, these are the assessments that the teacher should re-administer if a student does not reach the recommended performance level.

Words in Context
Word Building
Long Vowel Review
Short Vowel Review

UNIT 8 By the Sea • **Lesson 5**

Rhyme Mime

[Teacher: This activity is about rhymes. I will say a rhyme, but I will leave one word out. Draw a line under the answer that best completes the rhyme.]

[Teacher: You eat a cake and fish in a _____.]

1.
  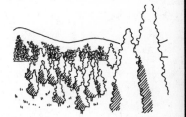

[Teacher: Tim is tall and he likes to play _____.]

2.
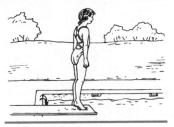  

[Teacher: I have fun when I play in the _____.]

3.

[Teacher: Beth is five and likes to_____.]

4.

[Teacher: Juan wants to know if it will _____.]

5.

UNIT 8   By the Sea • **Lesson 10**

Words in Context

[Teacher: This activity is about words and sentences. I will say a sentence, but I will blend one word. Draw a line under the word I blend.]

[Teacher: Ella saw a /b/ /u/ /g/. What did Ella see?]

1.

    cob   pig   <u>bug</u>

[Teacher: The /p/ /e/ /n/ was on the table. What was on the table?]

2.

    <u>pen</u>   pot   nut

[Teacher: The /c/ /a/ /t/ was black. What was black?]

3.

    <u>cat</u>   dog   bib

[Teacher: The /pl/ /u/ /m/ was purple. What was purple?]

4.

    pet   <u>plum</u>   hat

[Teacher: Paul used a /r/ /a/ /g/ to clean his car. What did Paul use?]

5.

    <u>rag</u>   mud   pan

UNIT 8   By the Sea • **Lesson 15**

High-Frequency Words

[Teacher: This activity is about words you have learned. Look at each group of words and listen to what I say. Draw a line under the word I say.]

[Teacher: The word is *here*. Draw a line under *here*.]

1.

have   here   has

[Teacher: The word is *who*. Draw a line under *who*.]

2.

what   when   who

[Teacher: The word is *like*. Draw a line under *like*.]

3.

like   look   too

[Teacher: The word is *small*. Draw a line under *small*.]

4.

see   small   she

[Teacher: The word is *this*. Draw a line under *this*.]

5.

that   the   this

LESSON ASSESSMENT

LESSON ASSESSMENT

UNIT 8 By the Sea• **Lesson 18**

Figurative Language

[Teacher: This activity is about figurative language, the way we describe things. Listen to what I say. Draw a line under the answer you think is right.]

[Teacher: Which of these is "as tall as a tree"?]

1.

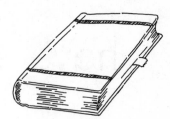

[Teacher: Which of these is "as fast as lightning"?]

2.

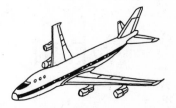

[Teacher: Which of these is "as soft as silk"?]

3.

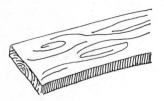
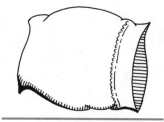

[Teacher: Which of these is "as light as a feather"?]

4.

[Teacher: Which of these is "as sweet as sugar"?]

5.

Name _____ Date _____ Score _____

Word Building

[Teacher: This activity is about building words. Listen to what I say. Draw a line under the answer you think is right.]

[Teacher: The word in the box is *at*. Which letter should you add to make the word *rat*?]

1.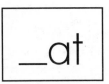

r   b   c

[Teacher: The word in the box is *or*. Which letter should you add to make the word *for*?]

2.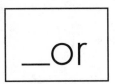

d   t   f

[Teacher: The word in the box is *top*. Which letter should you add to make the word *stop*?]

3.

c   s   z

[Teacher: The word in the box is *lay*. Which letter should you add to make the word *play*?]

4.

c   p   t

[Teacher: The word in the box is *lock*. Which letter should you add to make the word *clock*?]

5.

c   f   d

LESSON ASSESSMENT

UNIT 8 By the Sea

Long Vowel Review

[Teacher: This activity is about letter sounds. Listen carefully to what I say. Draw a line under the letter you think is right.]

[Teacher: The word in the box is *mine*. Which letter is missing from the word *mine*?]

1.    e   o   <u>i</u>

[Teacher: The word in the box is *mule*. Which letter is missing from the word *mule*?]

2.    <u>u</u>   i   o

[Teacher: The word in the box is *late*. Which letter is missing from the word *late*?]

3.   i   <u>a</u>   u

[Teacher: The word in the box is *me*. Which letter is missing from the word *me*?]

4.    <u>e</u>   o   a

[Teacher: The word in the box is *rode*. Which letter is missing from the word *rode*?]

5. 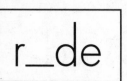   i   <u>o</u>   e

UNIT 8 By the Sea

Short Vowel Review

[Teacher: This activity is about letter sounds. Listen carefully to what I say. Draw a line under the letter you think is right.]

[Teacher: The word in the box is *cut*. Which letter is missing from the word *cut*?]

1. 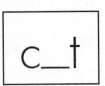   i   a   u̲

[Teacher: The word in the box is *had*. Which letter is missing from the word *had*?]

2. 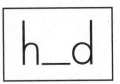   e   o   a̲

[Teacher: The word in the box is *got*. Which letter is missing from the word *got*?]

3. 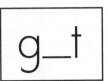   e   o̲   i

[Teacher: The word in the box is *tip*. Which letter is missing from the word *tip*?]

4.    i̲   o   e

[Teacher: The word in the box is *set*. Which letter is missing from the word *set*?]

5.   i   o   e̲

END OF UNIT ASSESSMENT

UNIT 1 School

Class Assessment Record

Student Name	Counting	Counting	Classifying and Categorizing	Classifying and Categorizing	Phonemic Awareness: Word Sequence	Rhyming Words	Colors	Shapes	Differentiating Words, Numbers, and Letters	Print and Book Awareness	Measurement Words

Class Assessment Record

Student Name	Position Words	Opposites	Vocabulary	Number Recognition	Letter Recognition (Capital)	Letter Recognition (Small)	High-Frequency Words	Alphabet Sequence	Words That Name

Class Assessment Record

Student Name	Cause and Effect	Counting Words in Sentences	Picture-Text Relationship	Drawing Conclusions	Word Order in Sentences	High-Frequency Words	Word Length	Vocabulary	Fantasy and Reality	Letter Recognition (Capital)	Letter Recognition (Small)

Class Assessment Record

Student Name	Alphabet Sequence	Matching Capital and Small Letters	Action Words	End Punctuation Marks

Class Assessment Record

Student Name	Blending Word Parts	Sentence Boundaries	Compound Words	High-Frequency Words	Setting	Deleting Syllables	Compare and Contrast	Blending Initial Sounds	Vocabulary	Words That Describe

Class Assessment Record

Student Name	Days of the Week	Following Directions	Letter Sounds	High-Frequency Words	Vocabulary	Plot	Word Pairs	Letter Sounds	Long Vowel Sounds	Words That Describe

Class Assessment Record

Student Name	Beginning and Ending Sounds	Predicting	Listening for Problems	High-Frequency Words	Quotation Marks	Vocabulary	Letter Sounds	Sounds in Words	Words That Show Action

Class Assessment Record

Student Name	Main Idea	Phoneme Replacement	Letter Sounds	Vocabulary	Letter Sounds	High-Frequency Words	Capital Letters and End Marks

Class Assessment Record

Student Name	Counting Phonemes	Letter Sounds	Vocabulary	Letter Sounds	Pronouns

Class Assessment Record

Student Name	Rhyme Mime	Words in Context	High-Frequency Words	Figurative Language	Word Building	Long Vowel Review	Short Vowel Review

Student Assessment Record

Name _____

Teacher _____ Grade _____

Unit	Assessment Name	Date	Number Possible	Number Right	%

Student Assessment Record • Unit Assessment